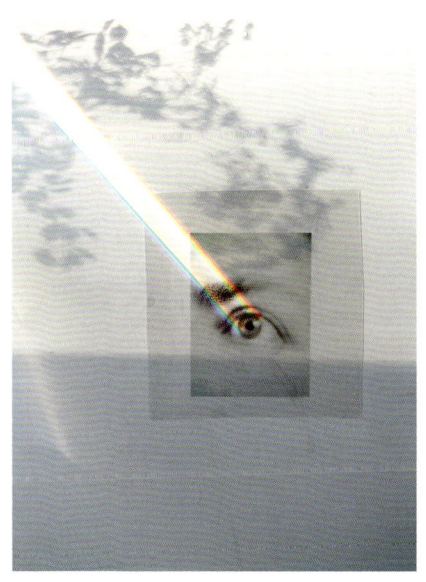

Cofounders: Taj Forer and Michael Itkoff
Creative Director: Ursula Damm

Photographs © 2019 by Jordanna Kalman
Her Power Arouses © 2019 by Jennifer Murray

ISBN 978-1-942084-73-0

Printed by Artron, China

Daylight Books
E-mail: info@daylightbooks.org
Web: www.daylightbooks.org

Little Romances

Jordanna Kalman

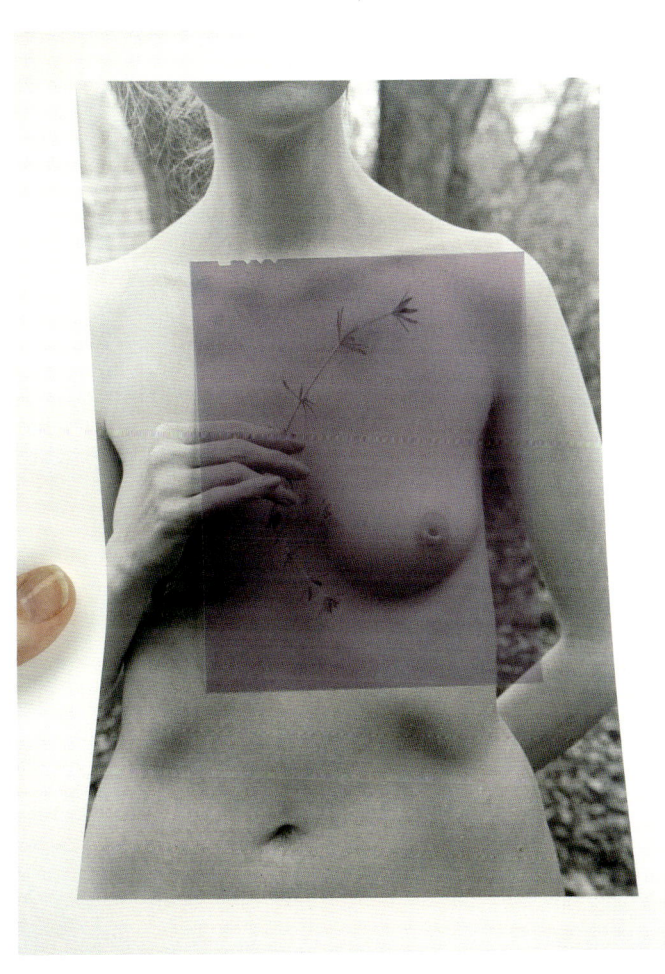

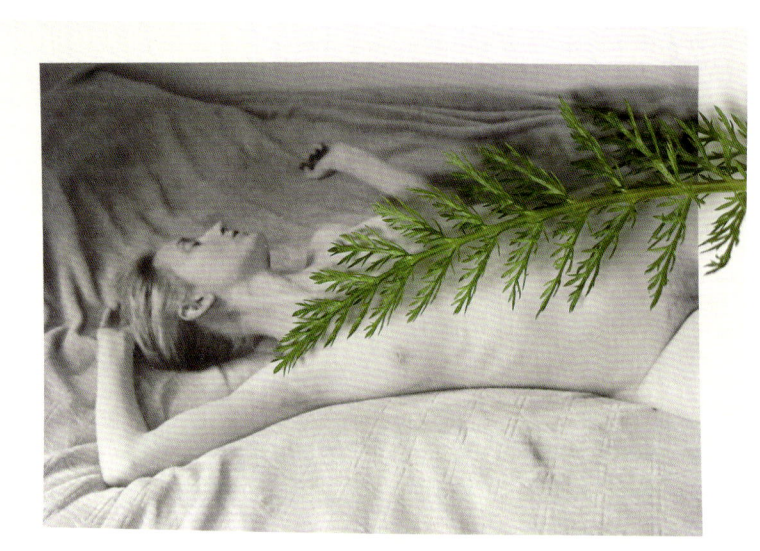

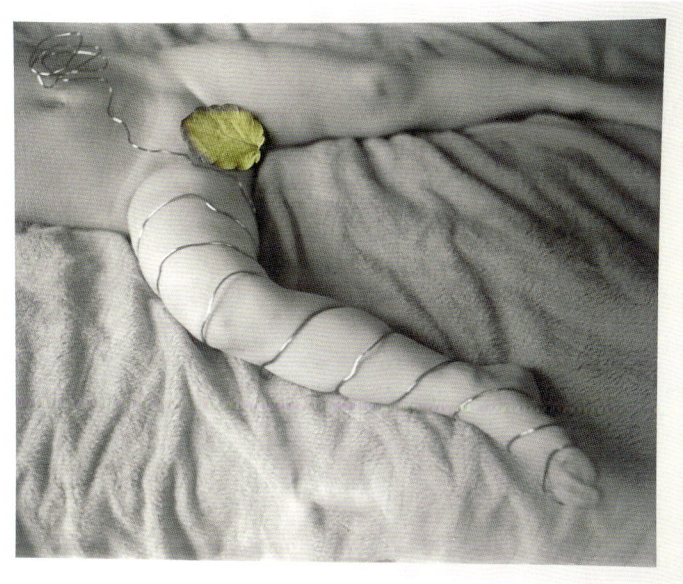

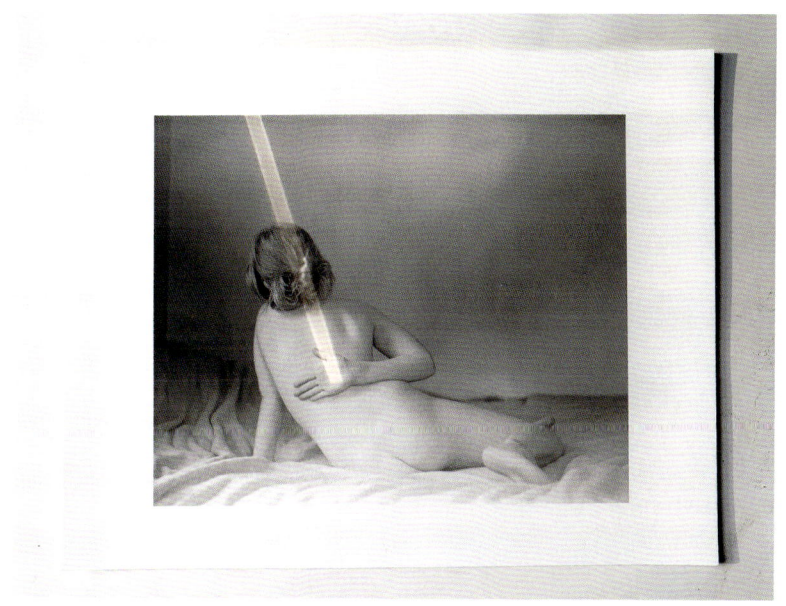

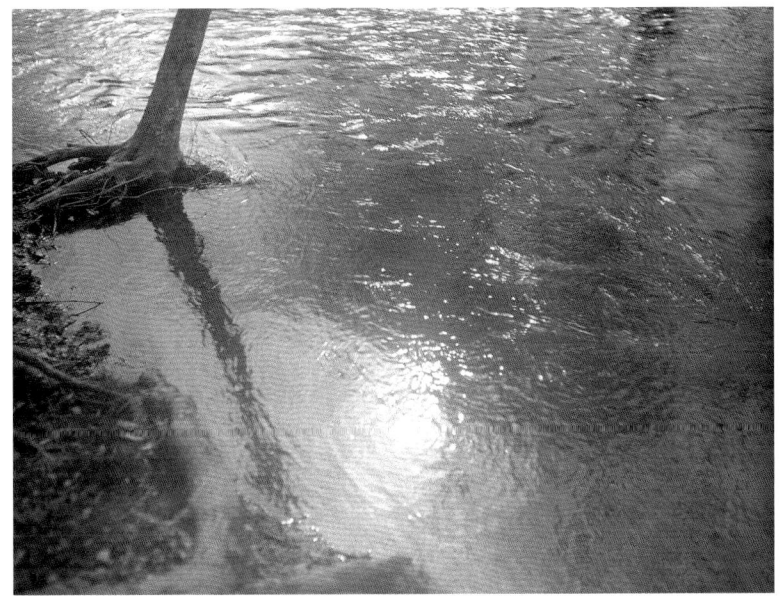

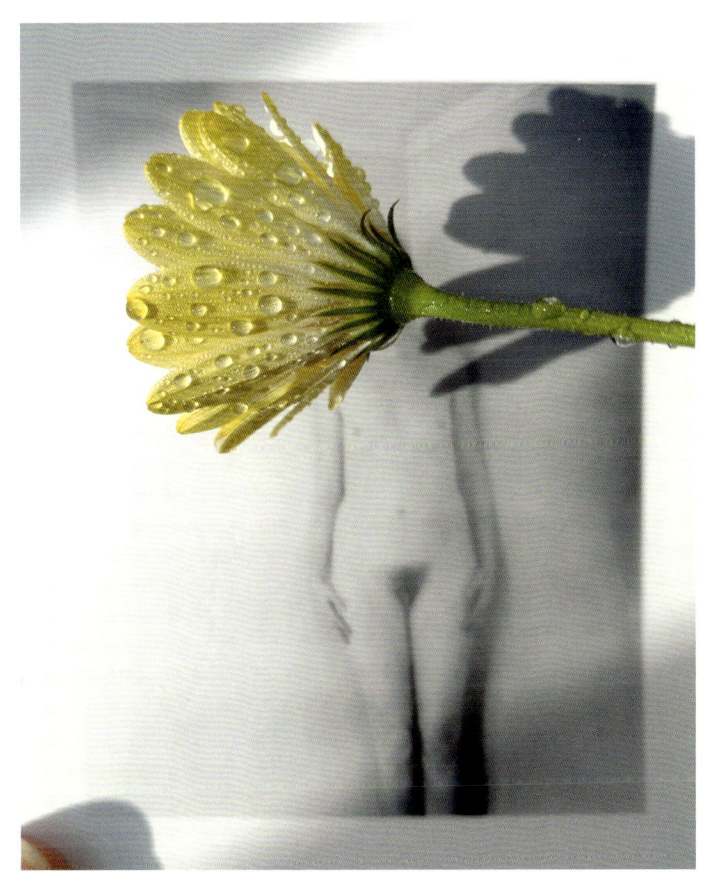

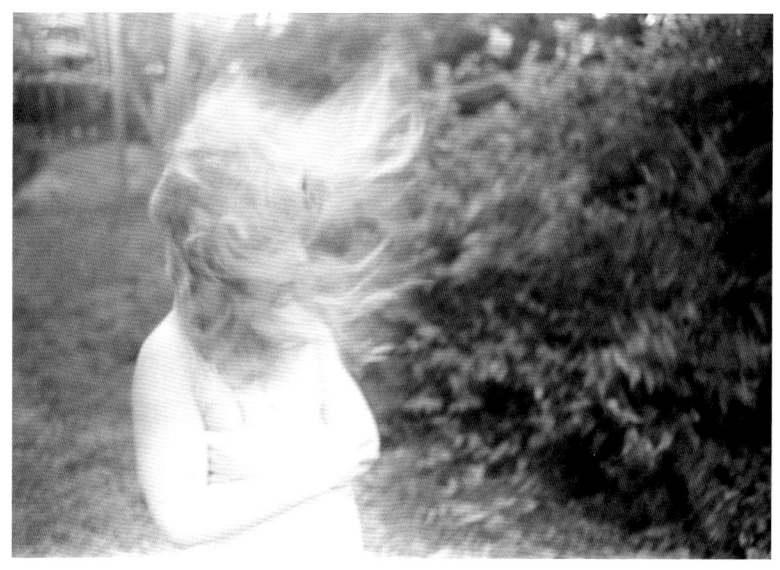

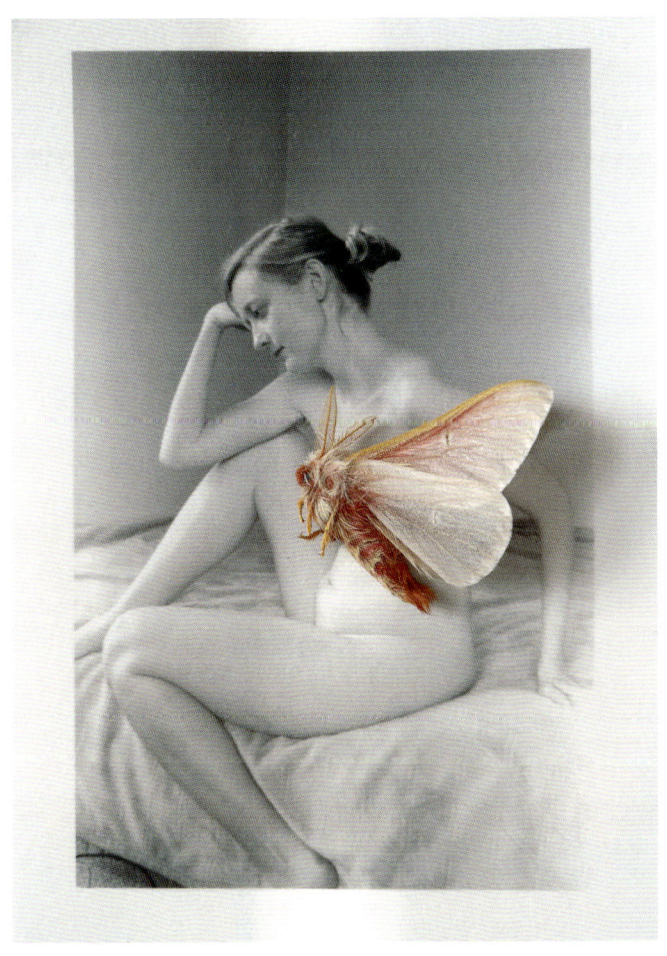

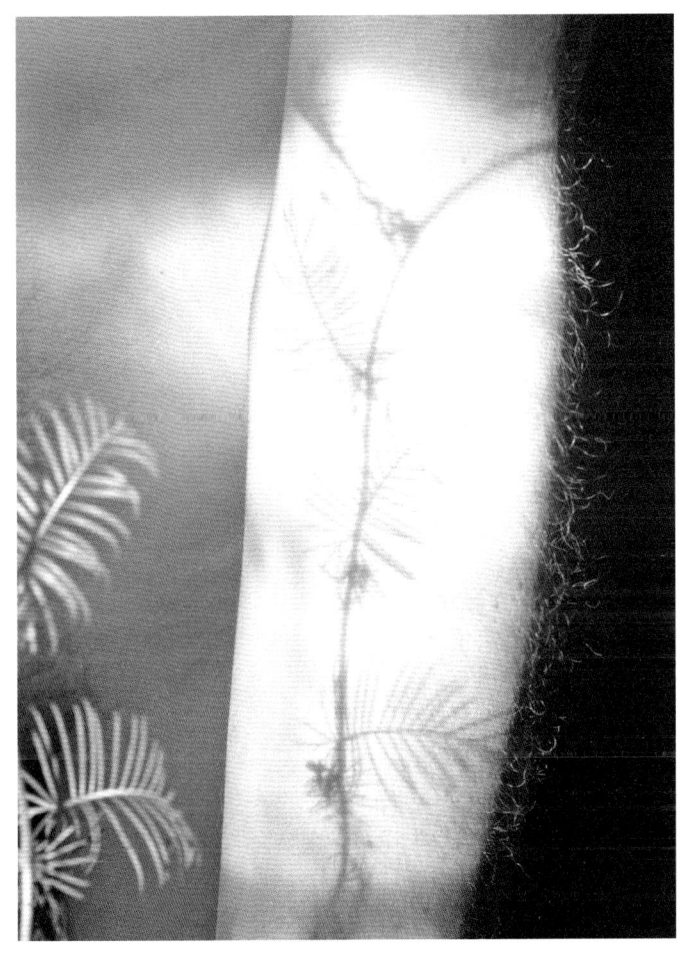

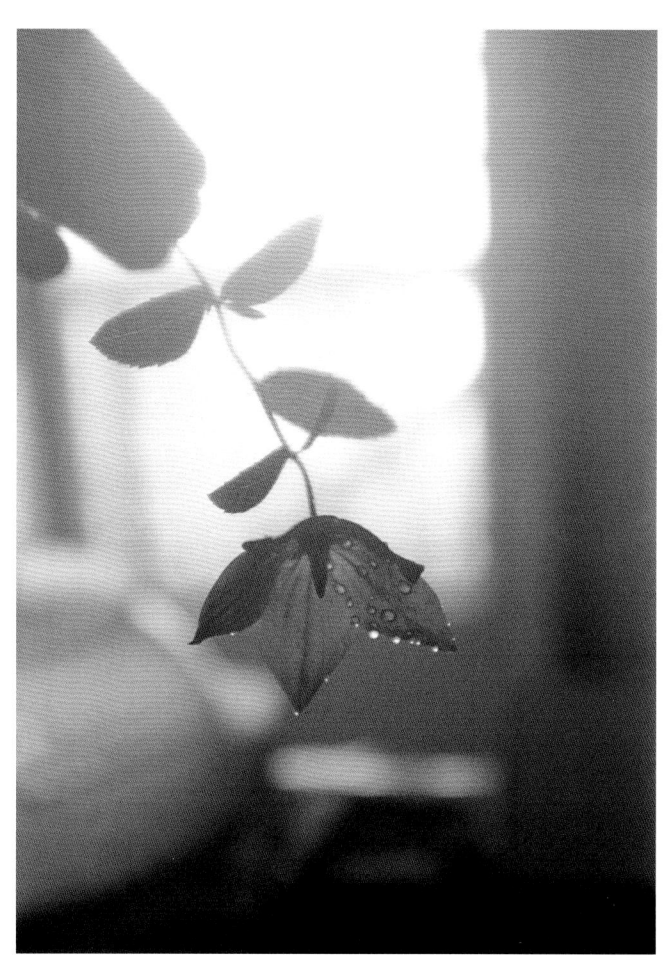

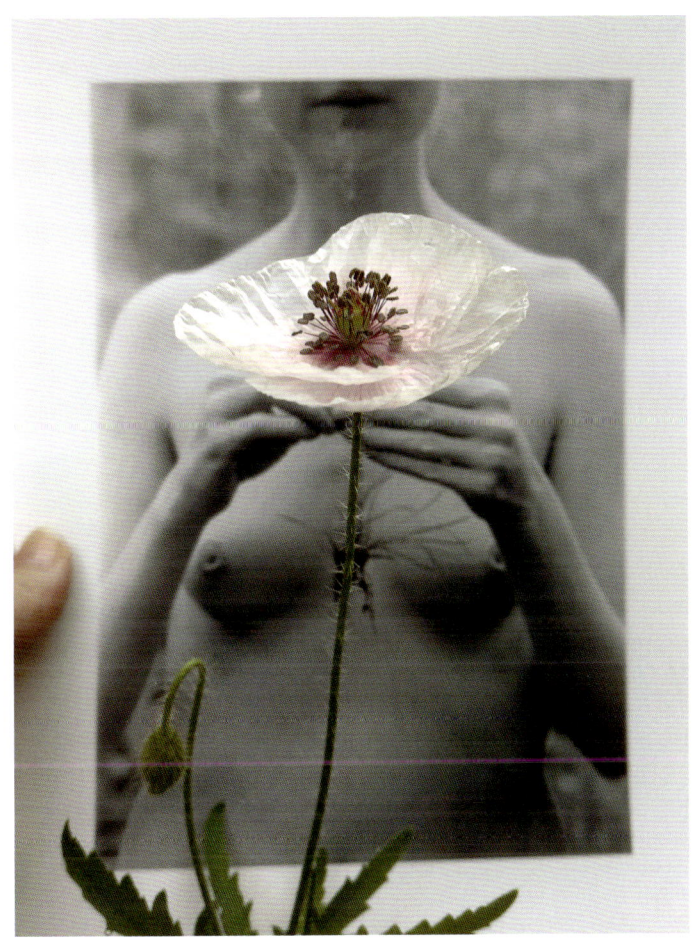

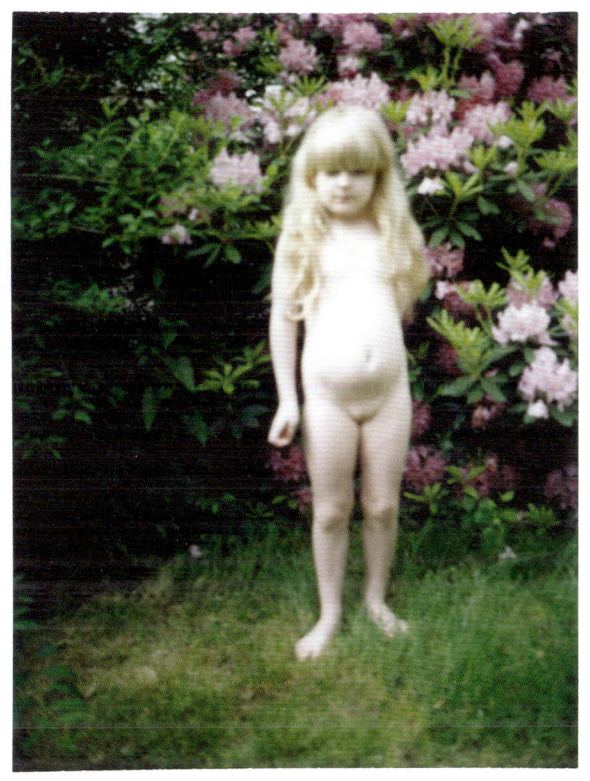

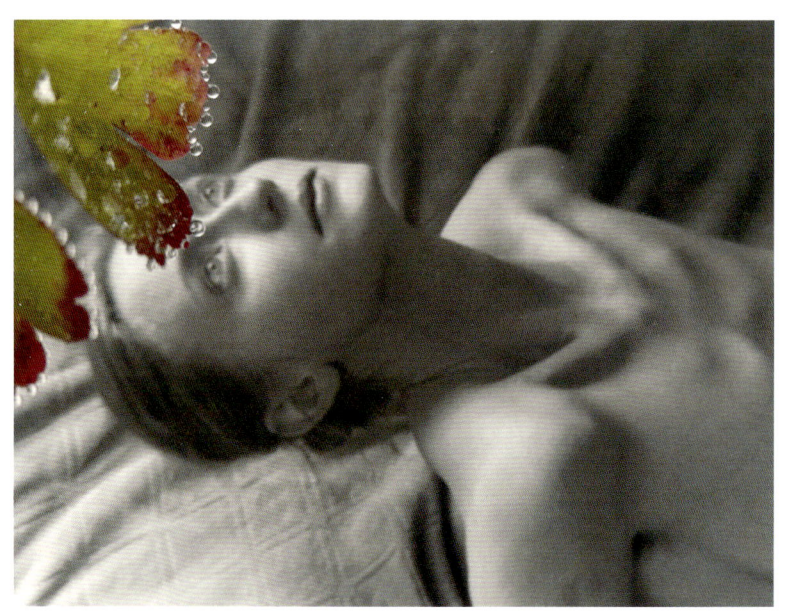

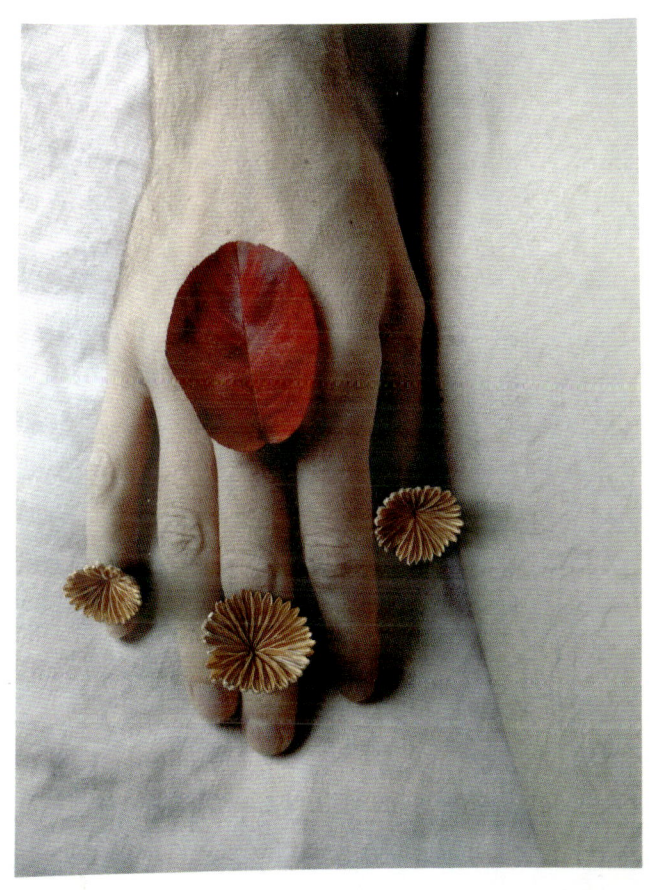

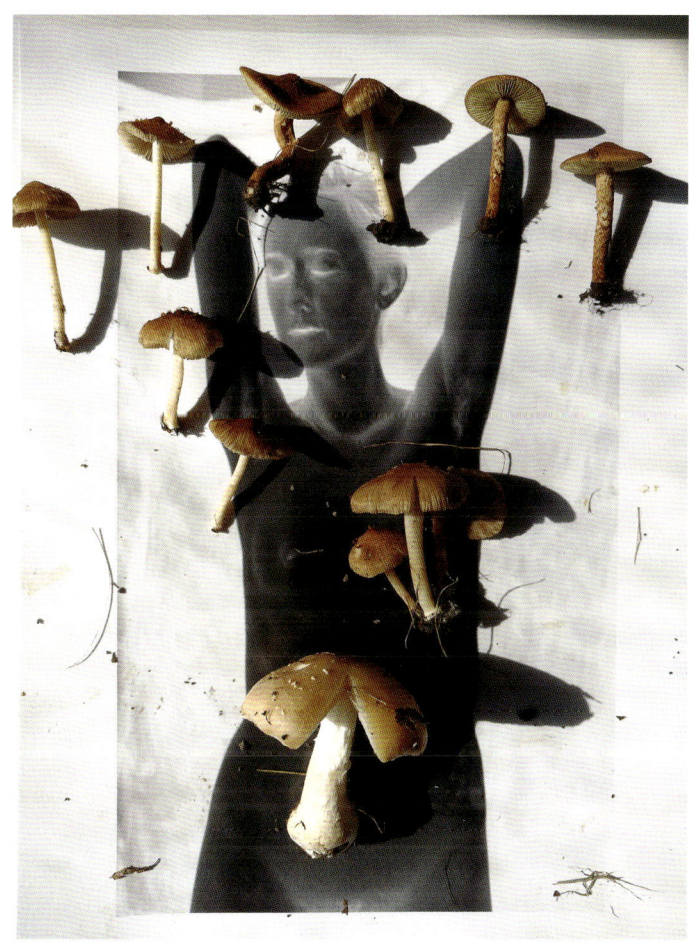

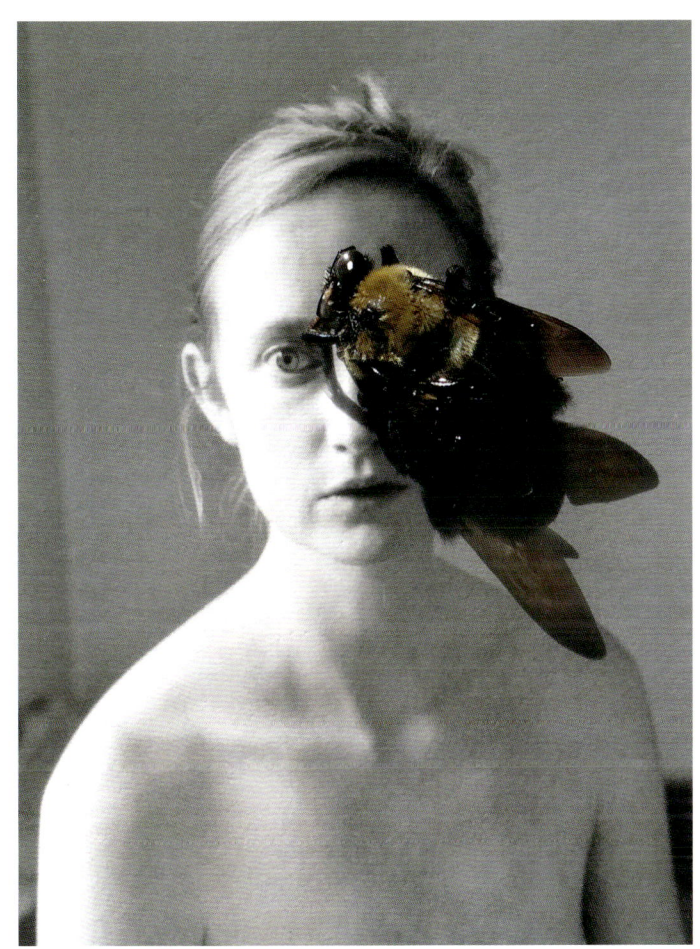

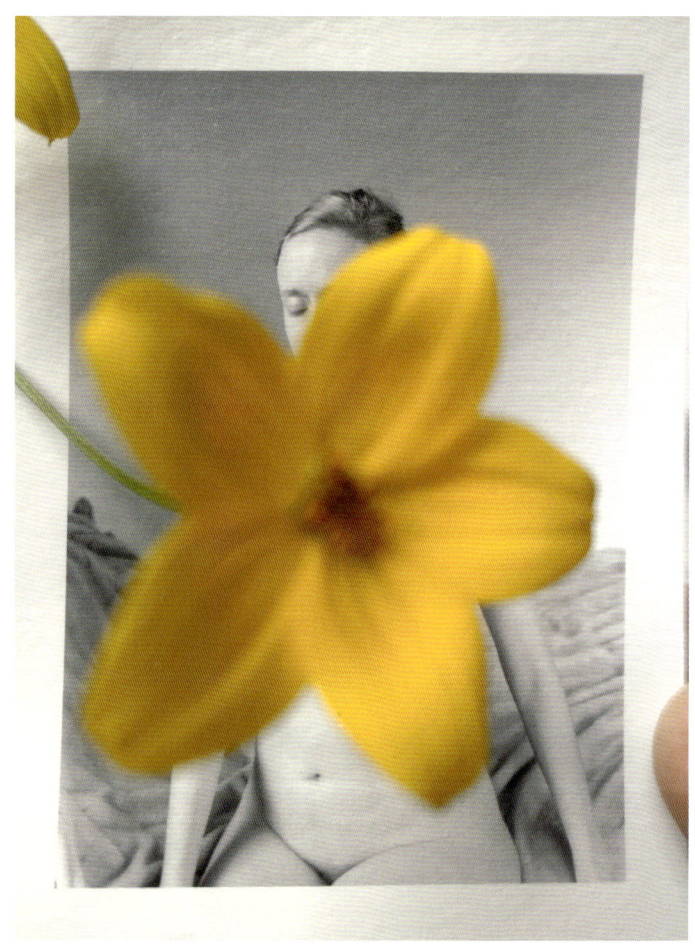

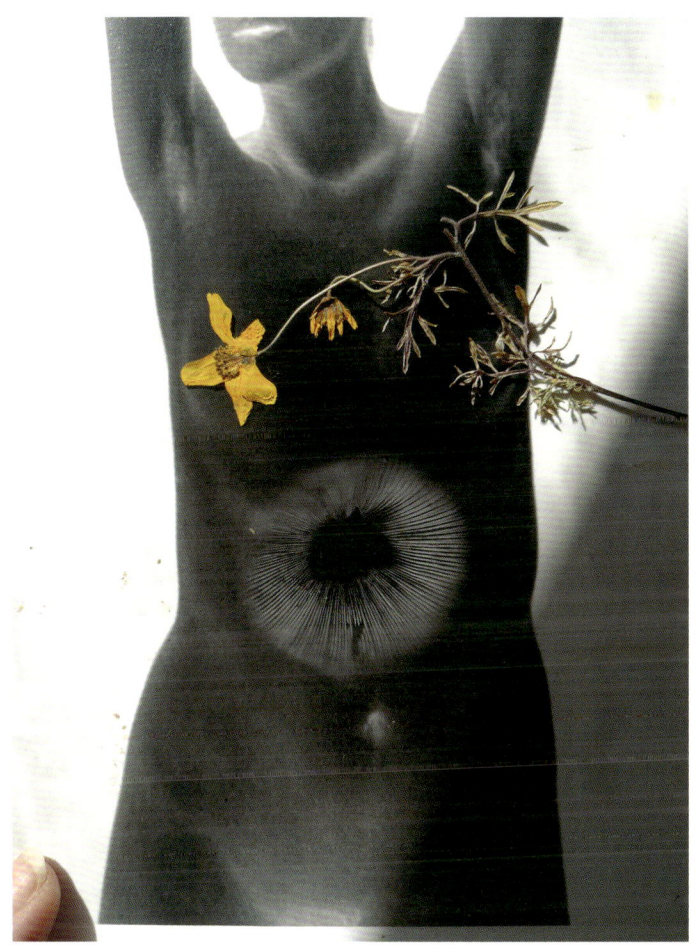

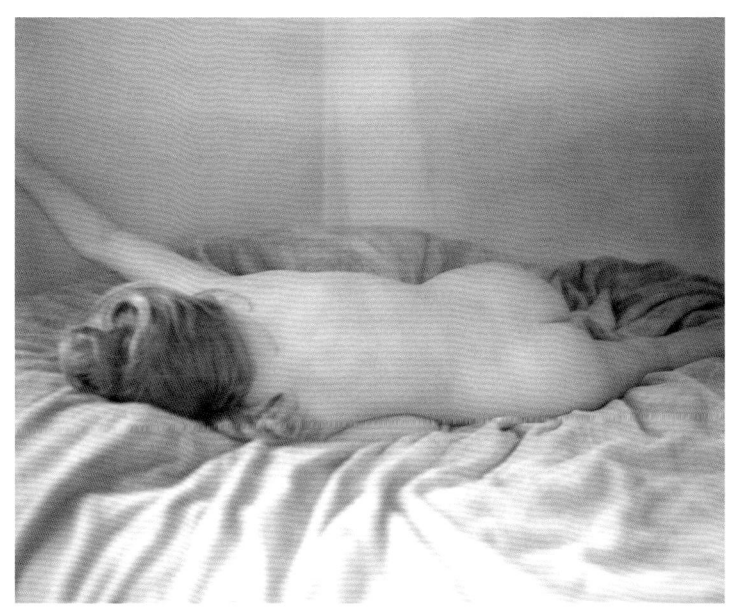

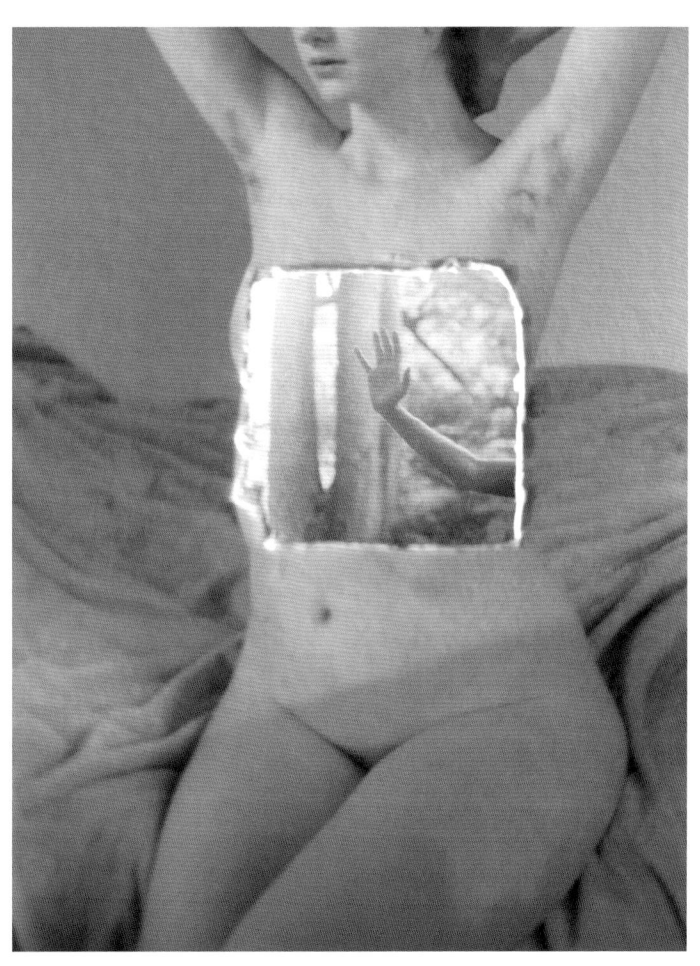

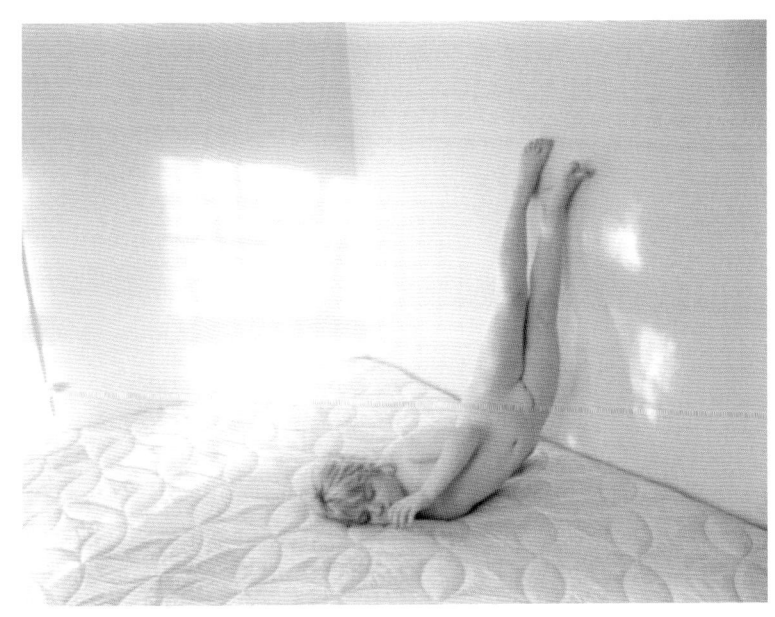

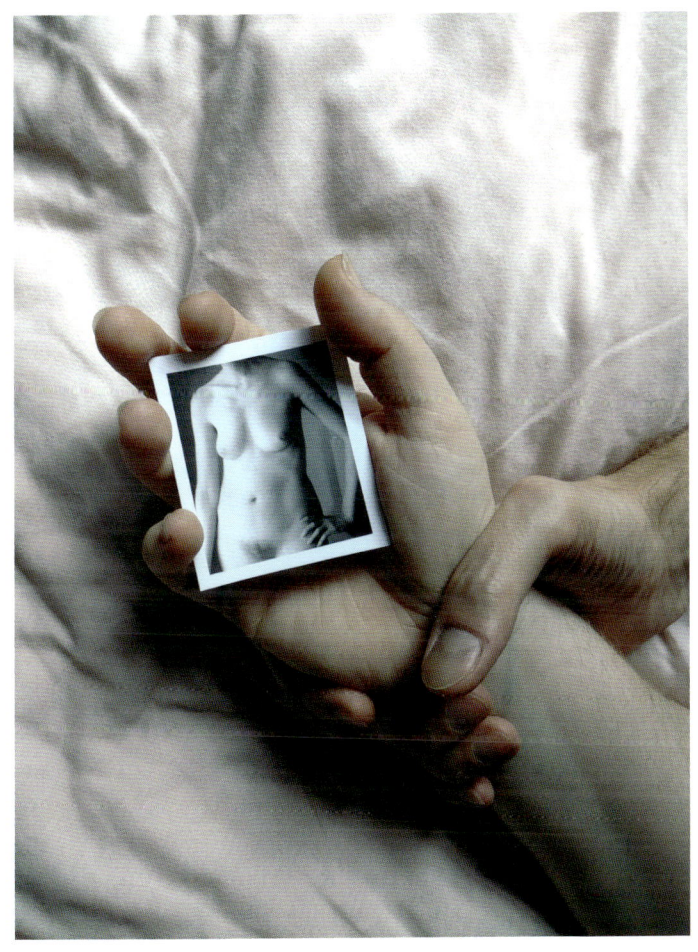

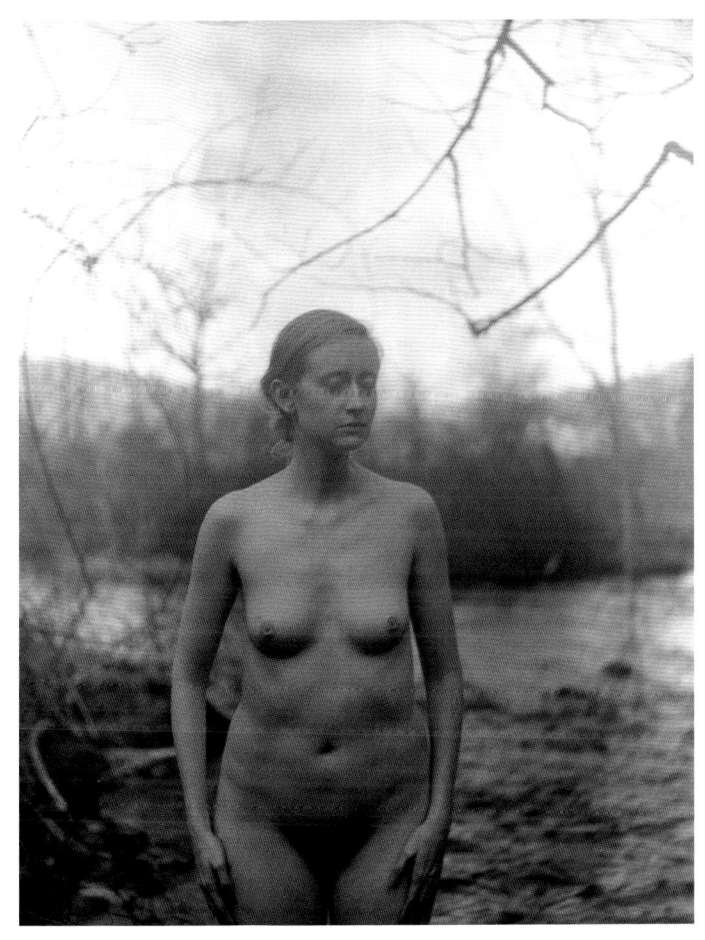

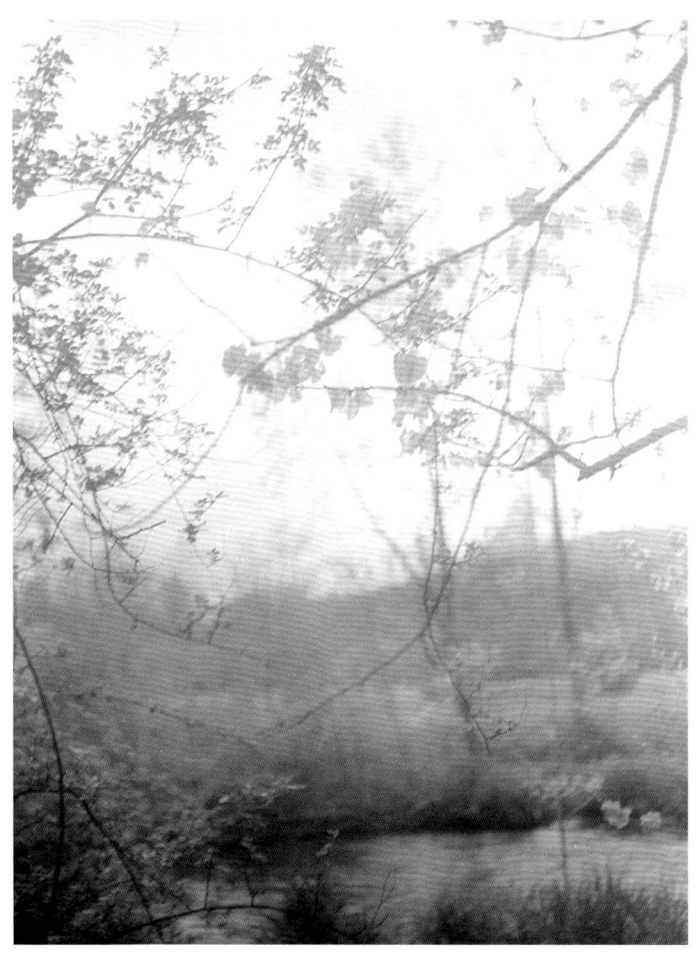

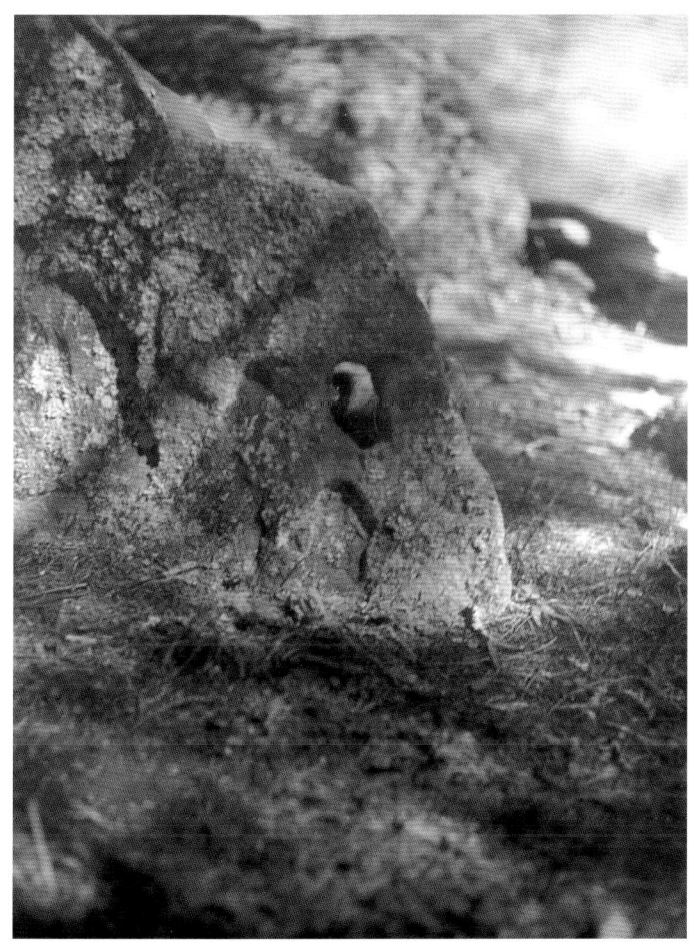

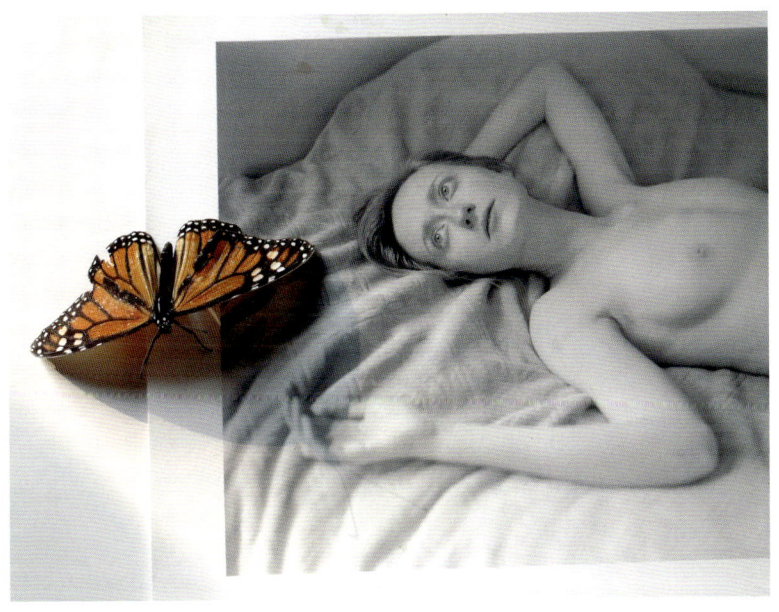

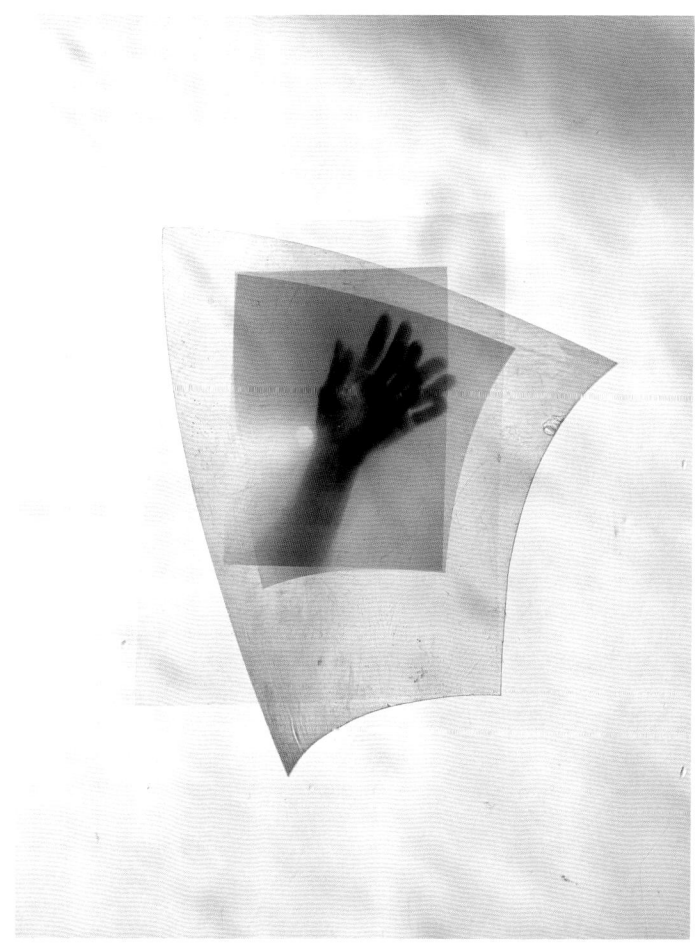

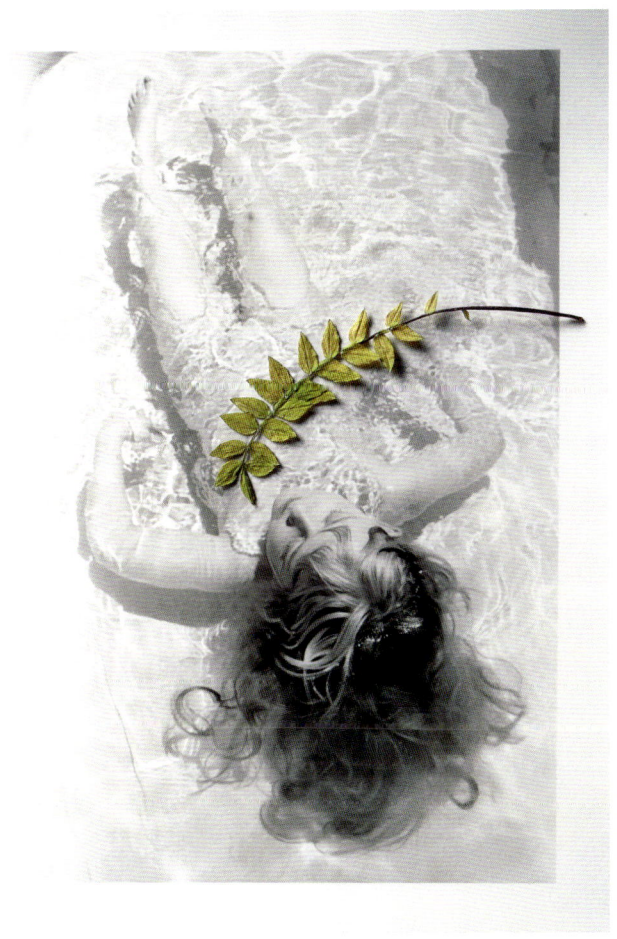

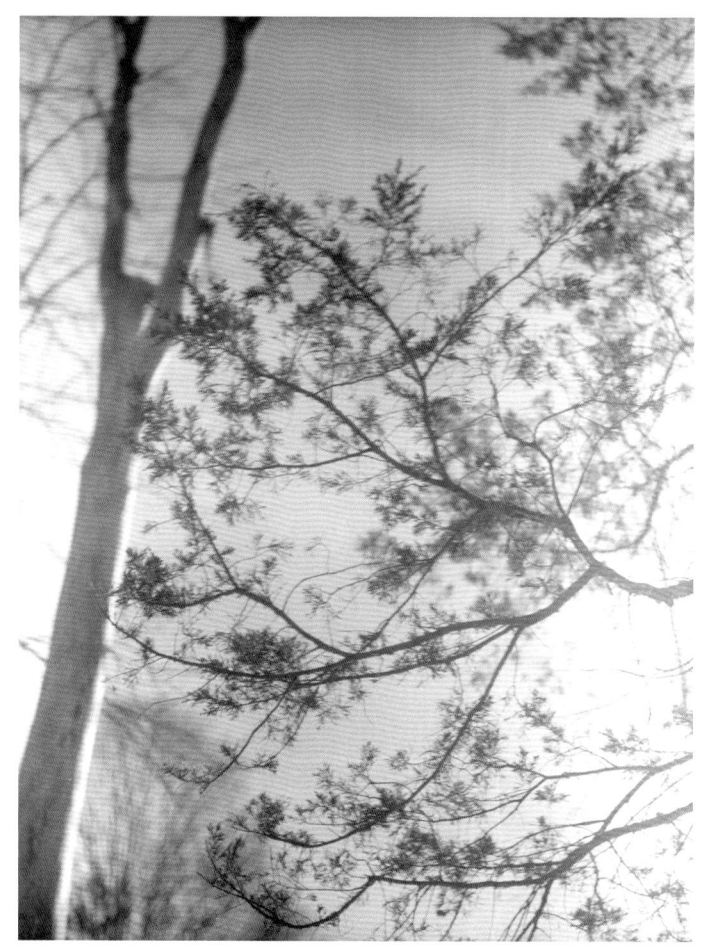

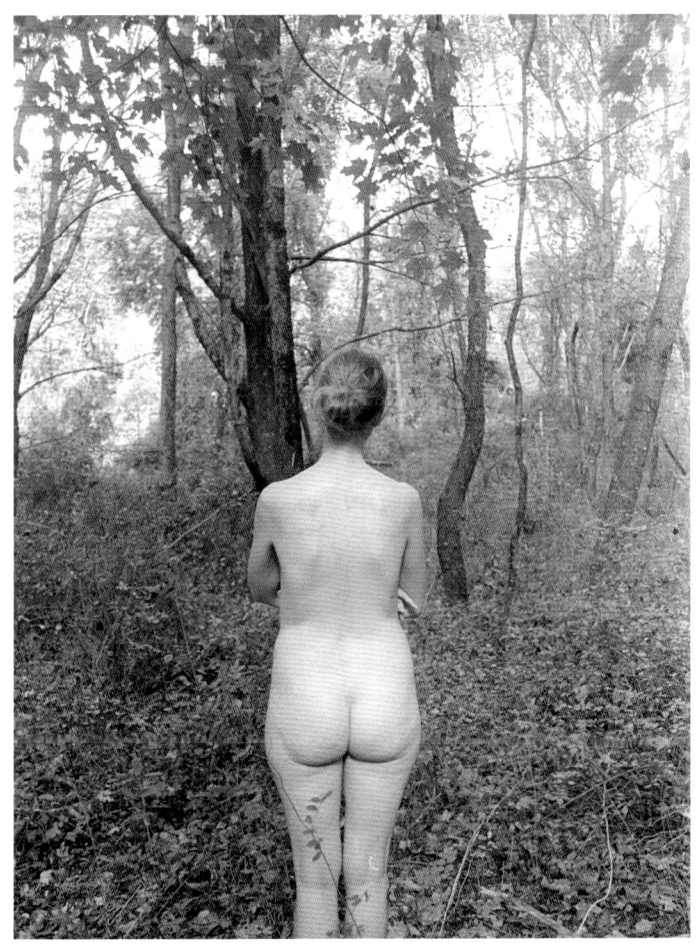

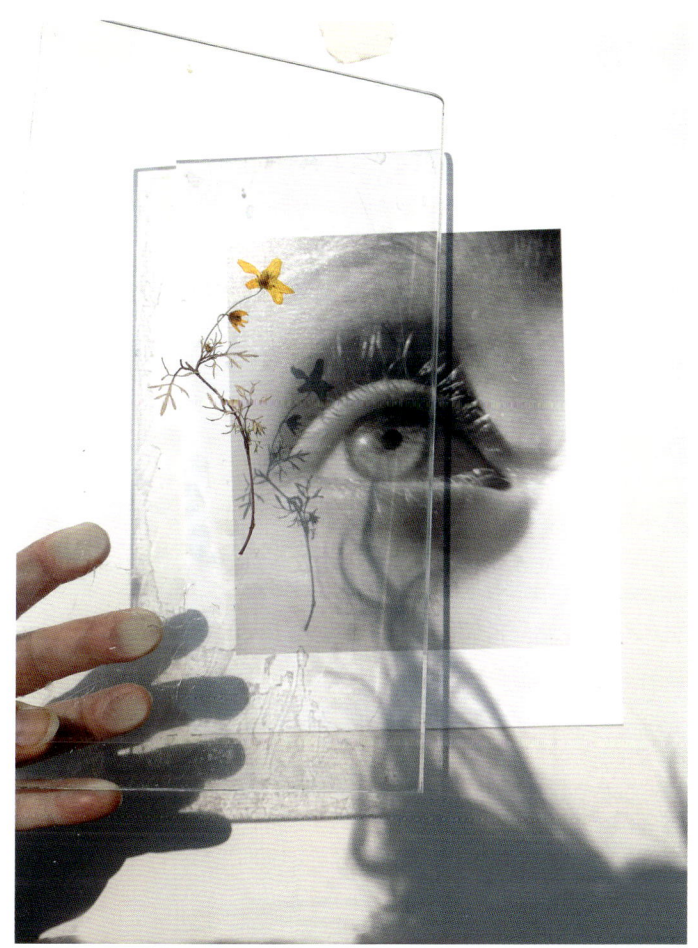

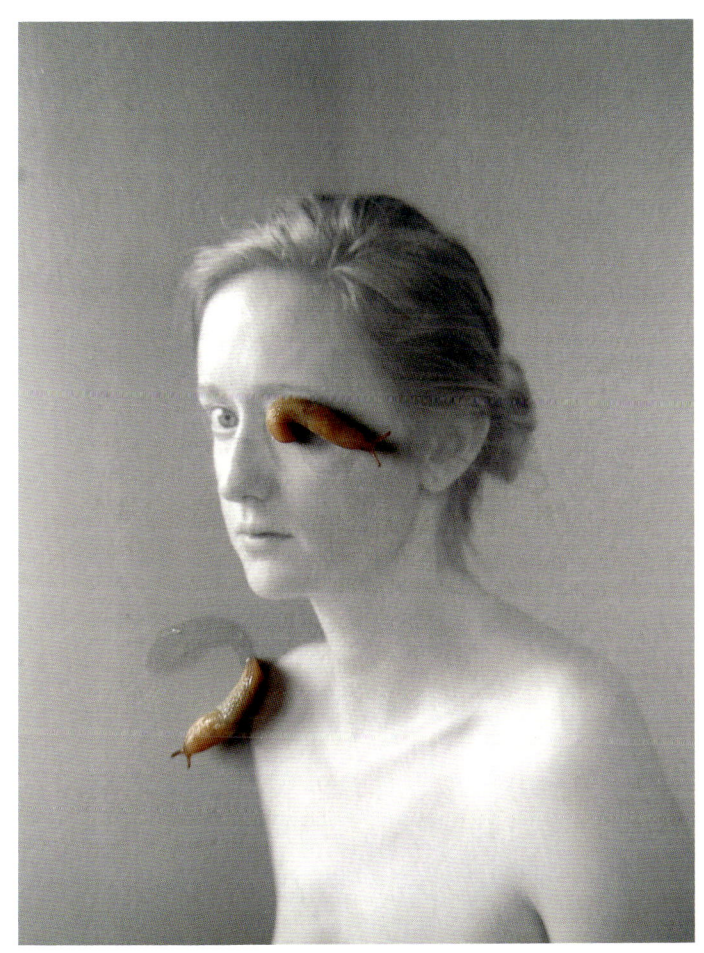

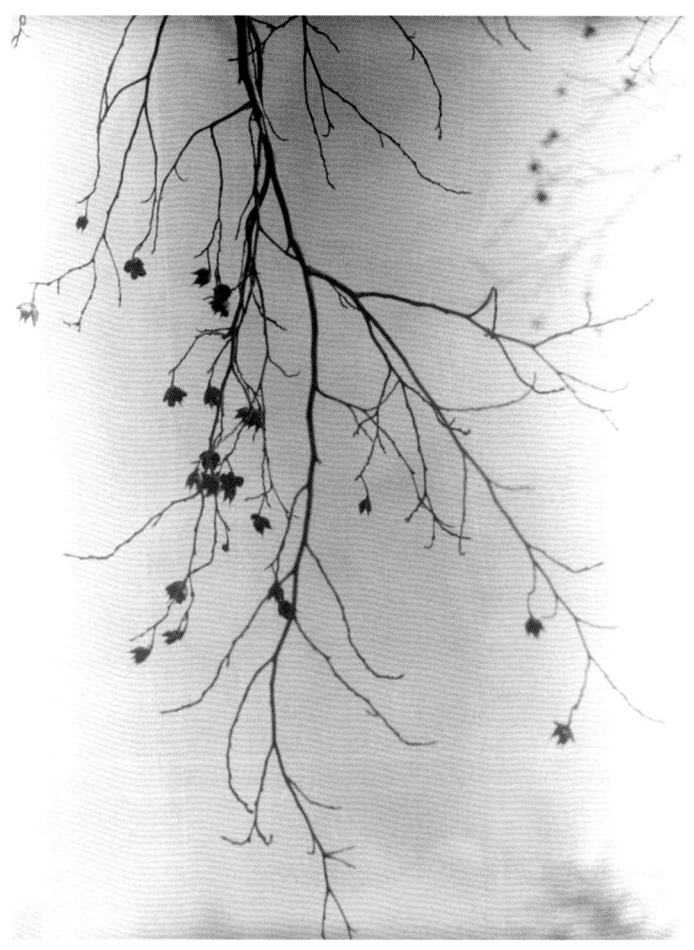

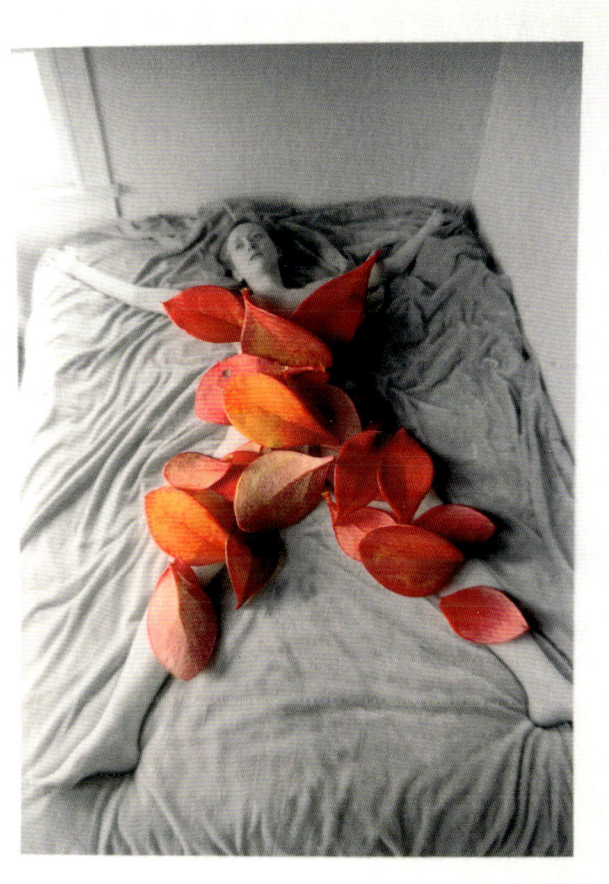

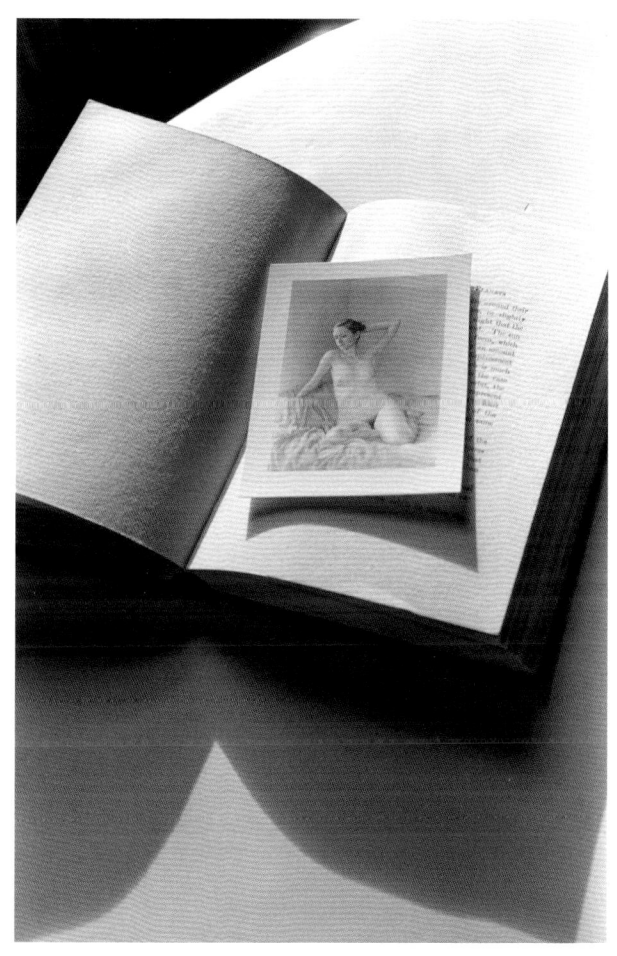

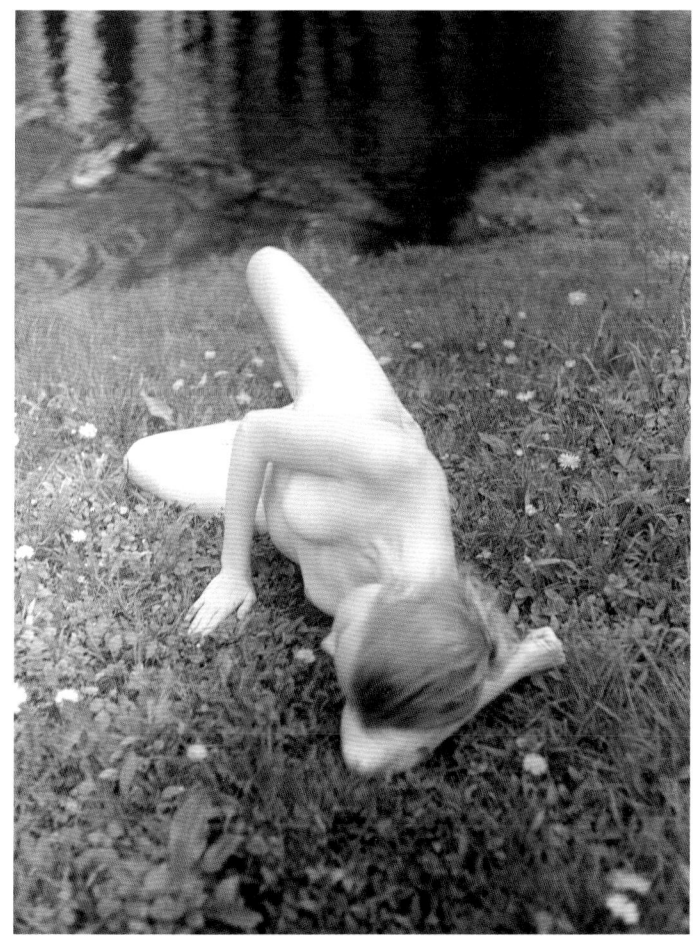

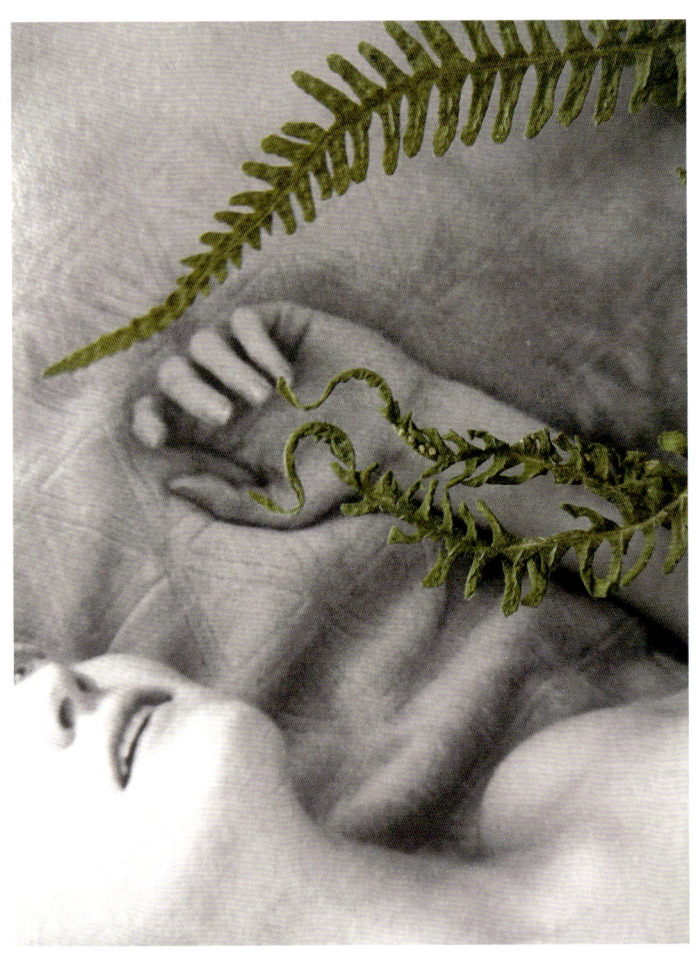

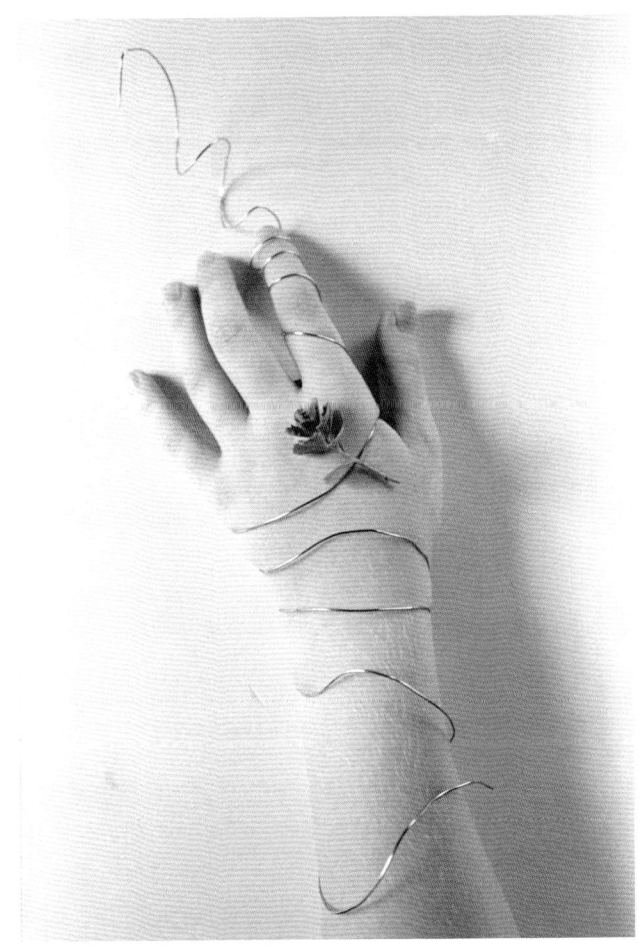

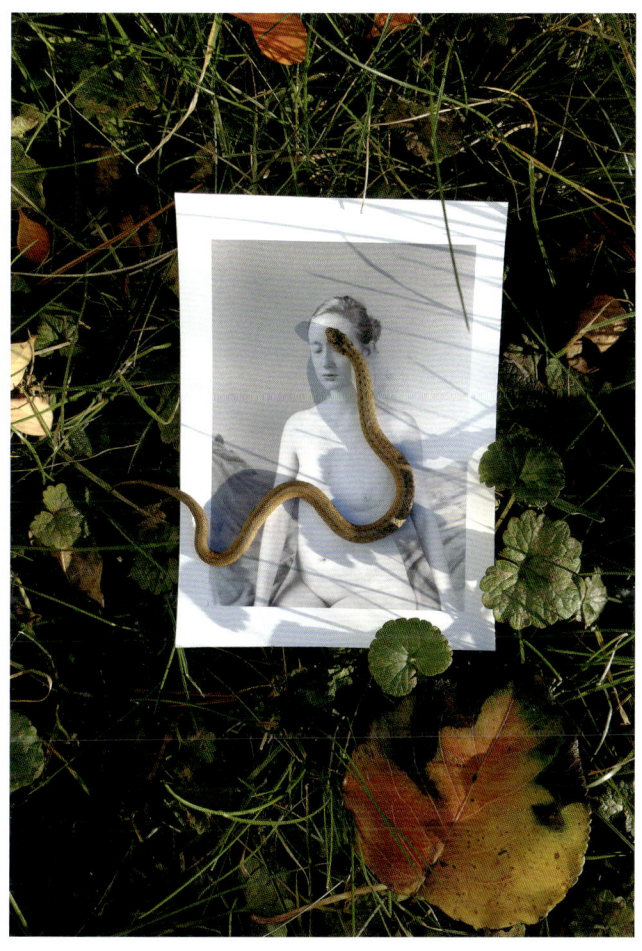

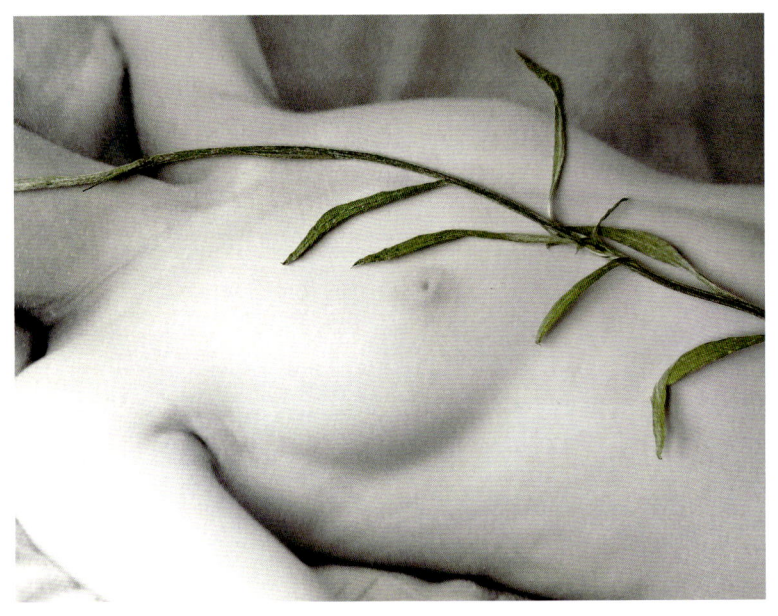

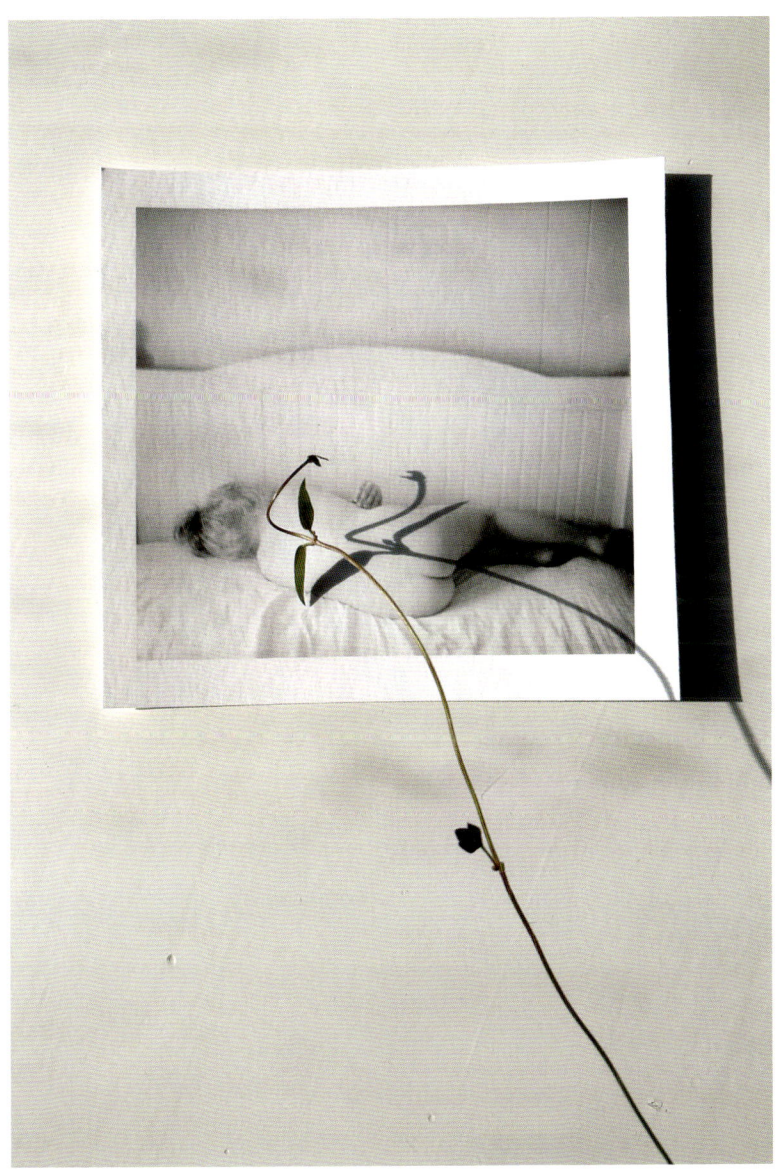

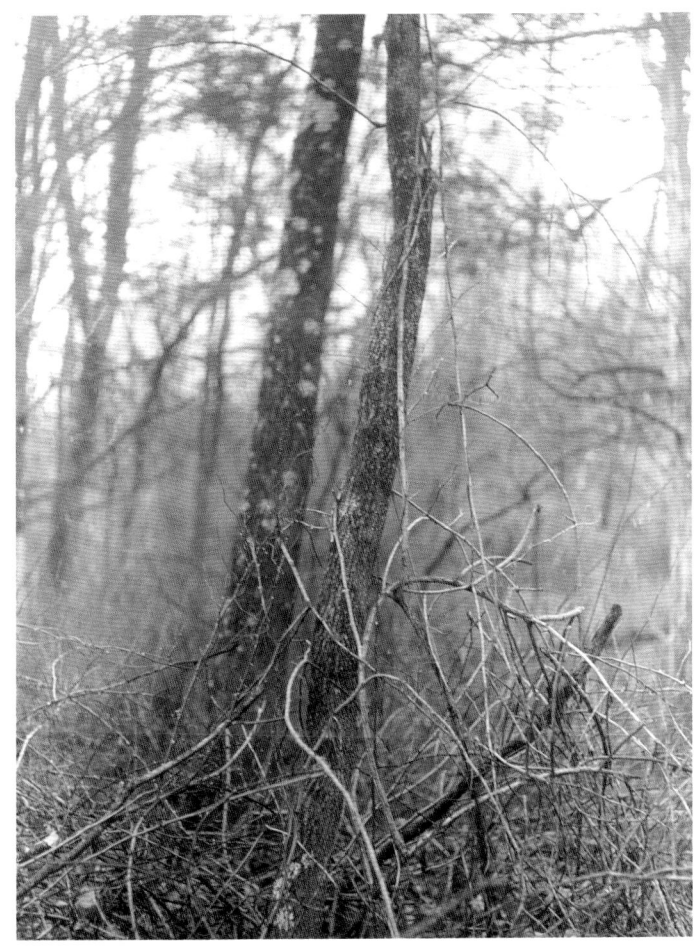

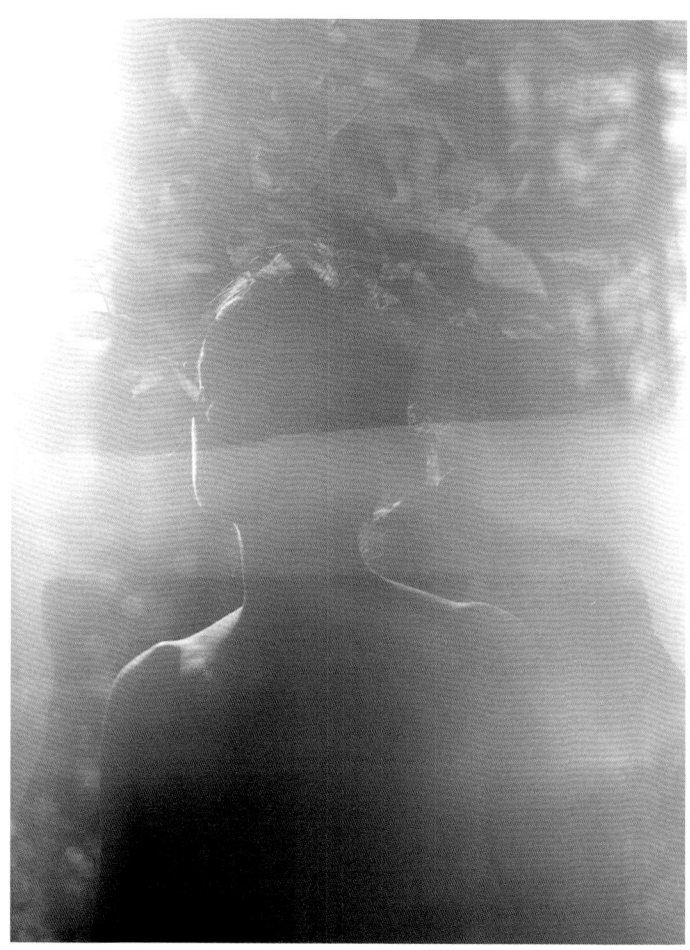

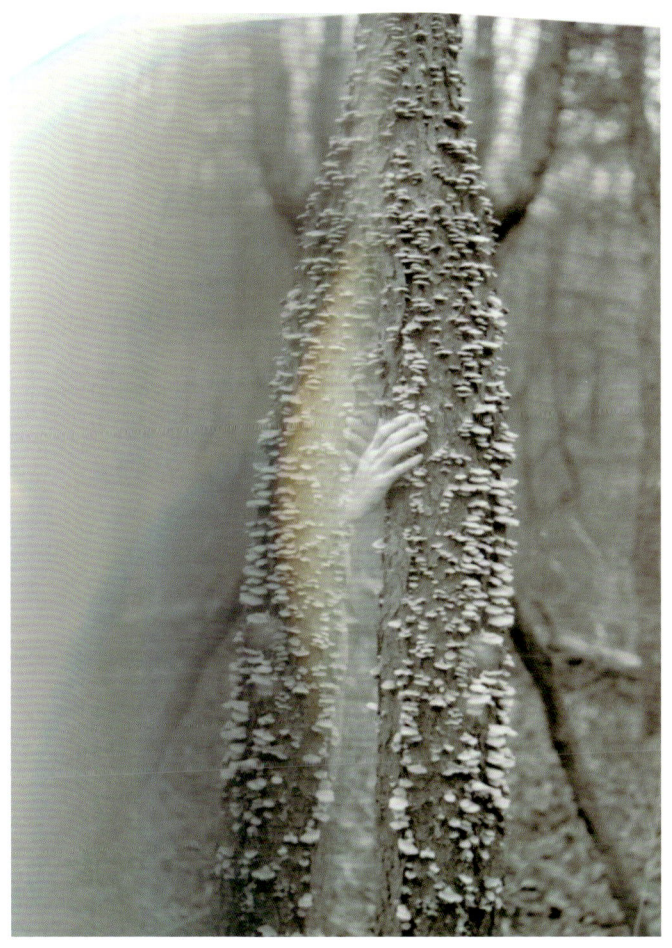

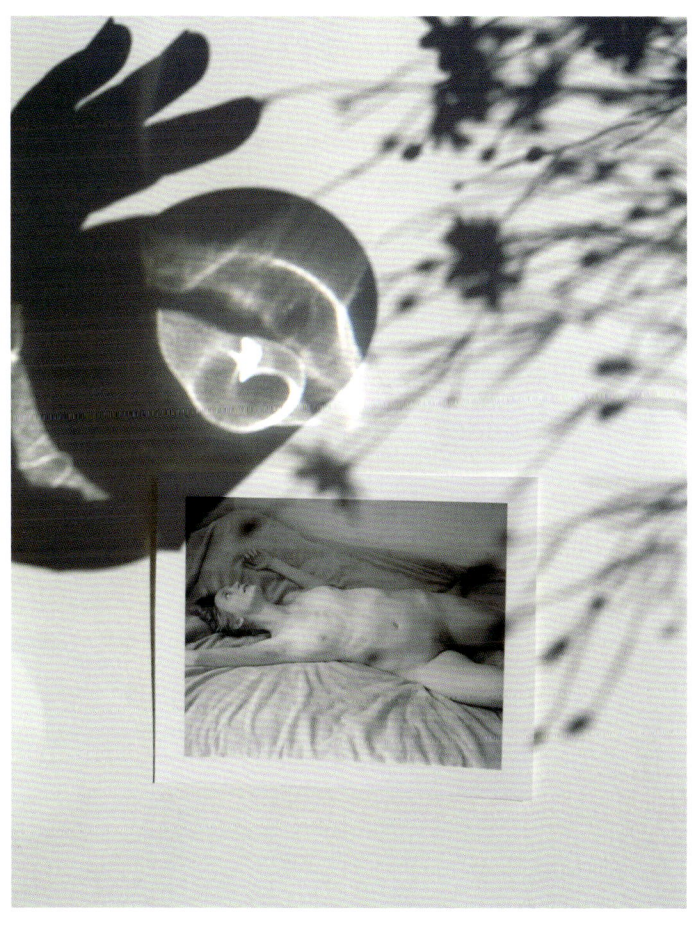

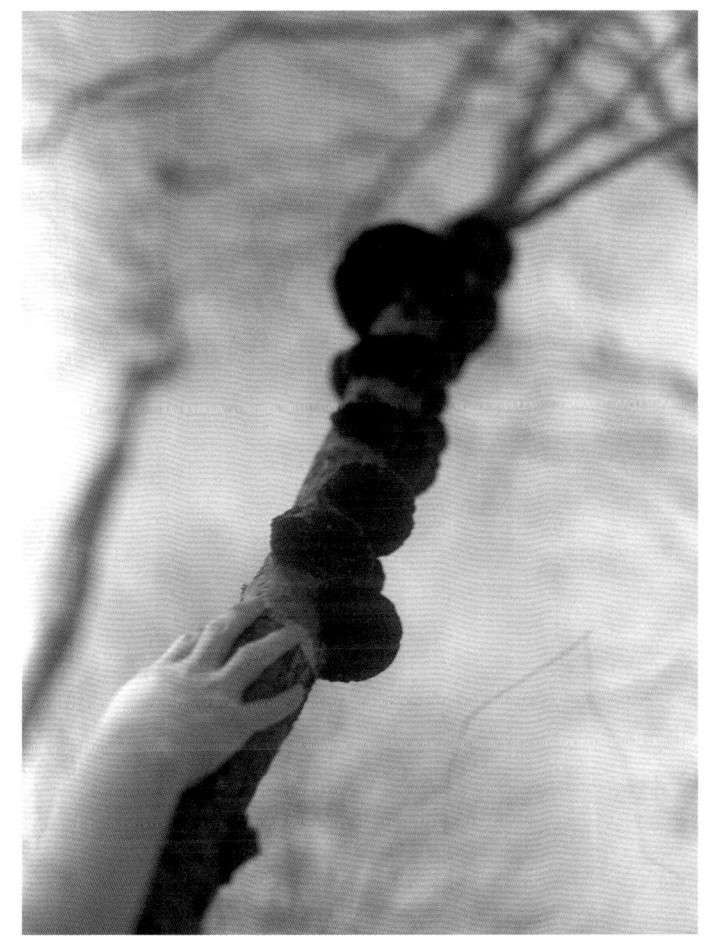

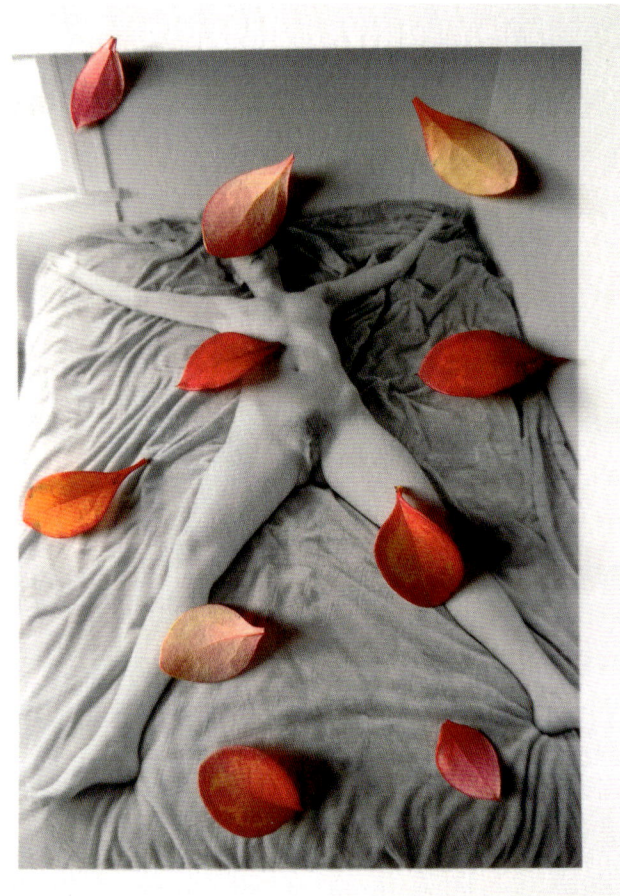

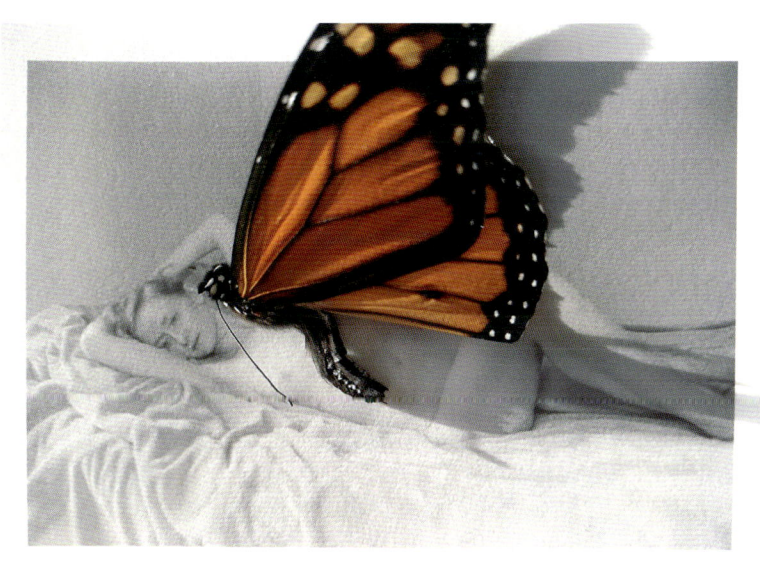

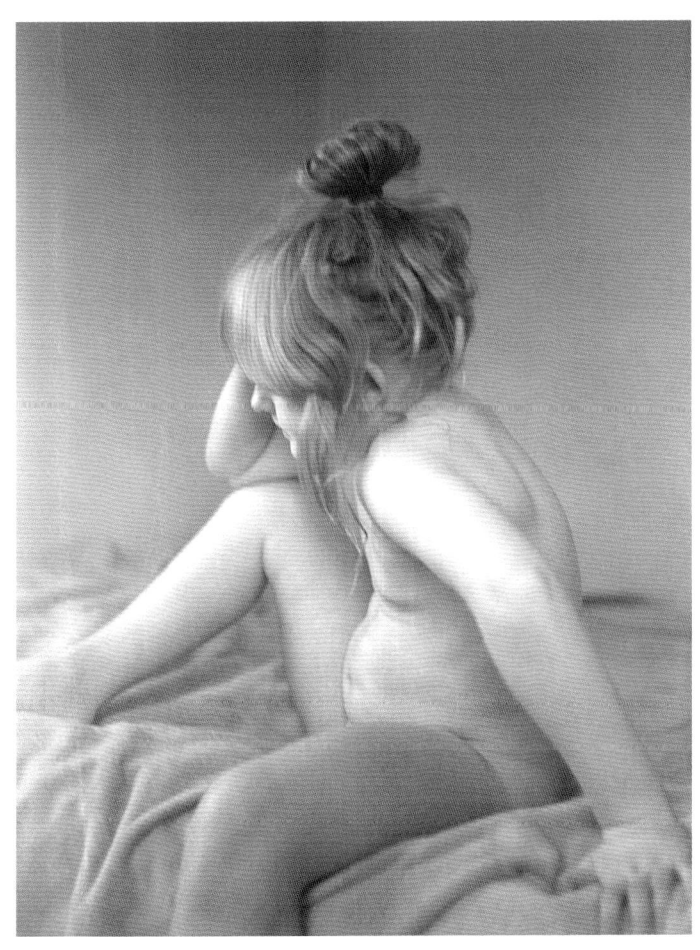

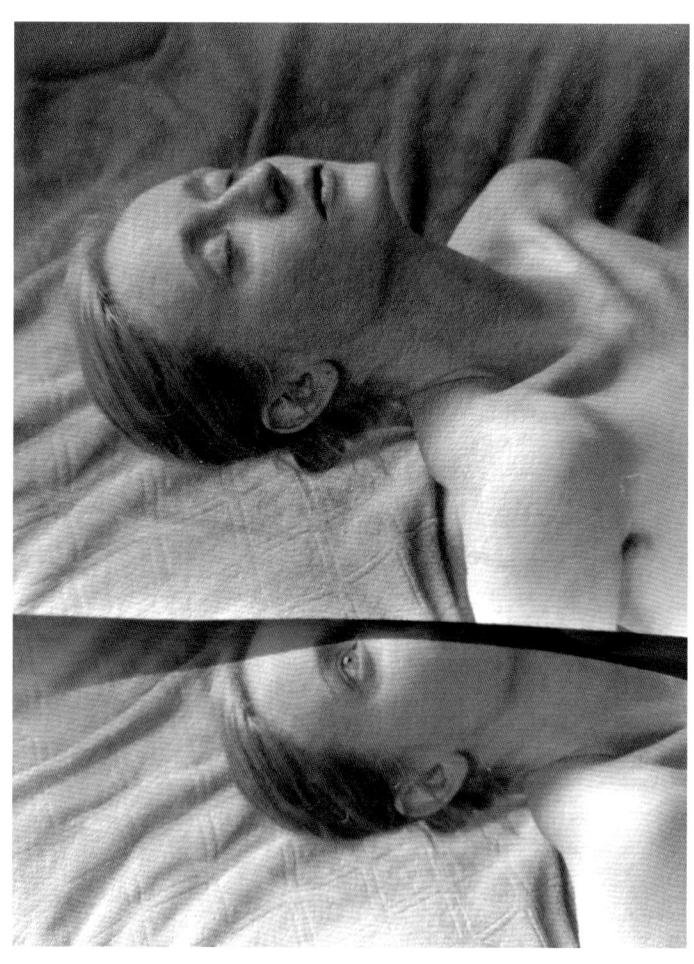

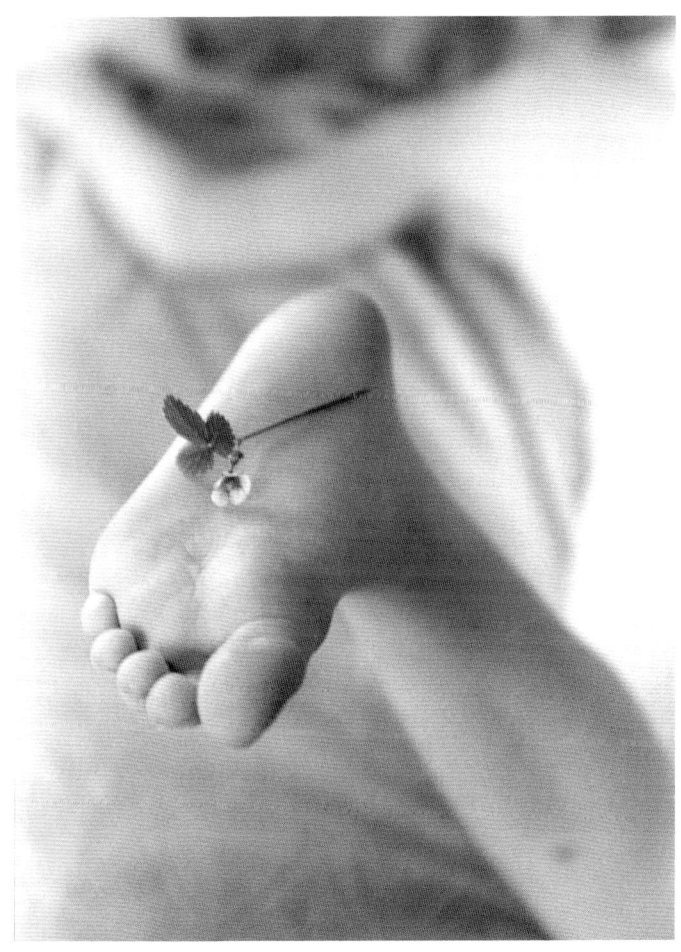

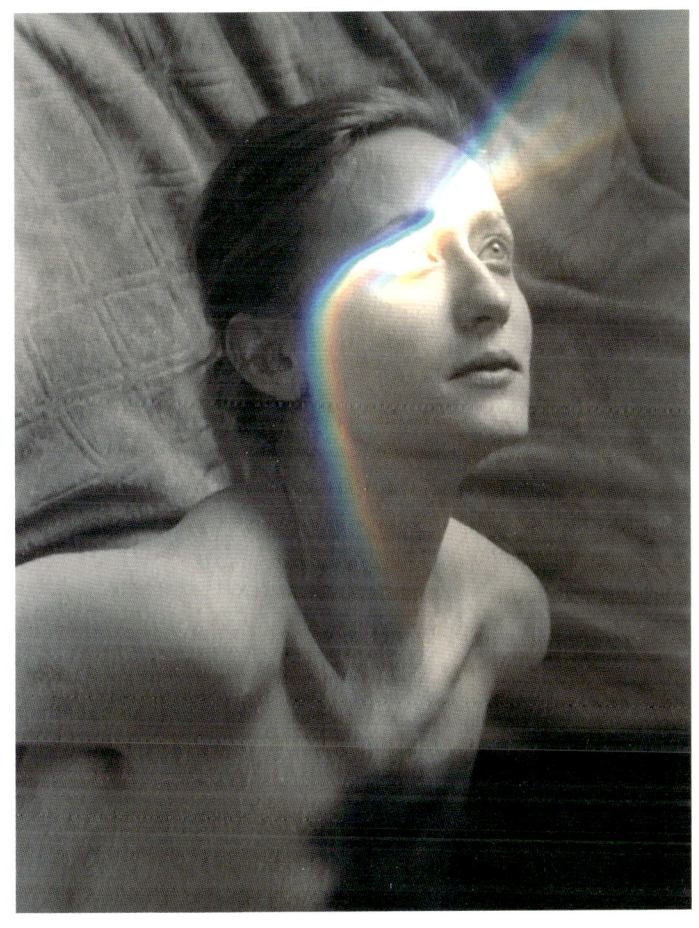

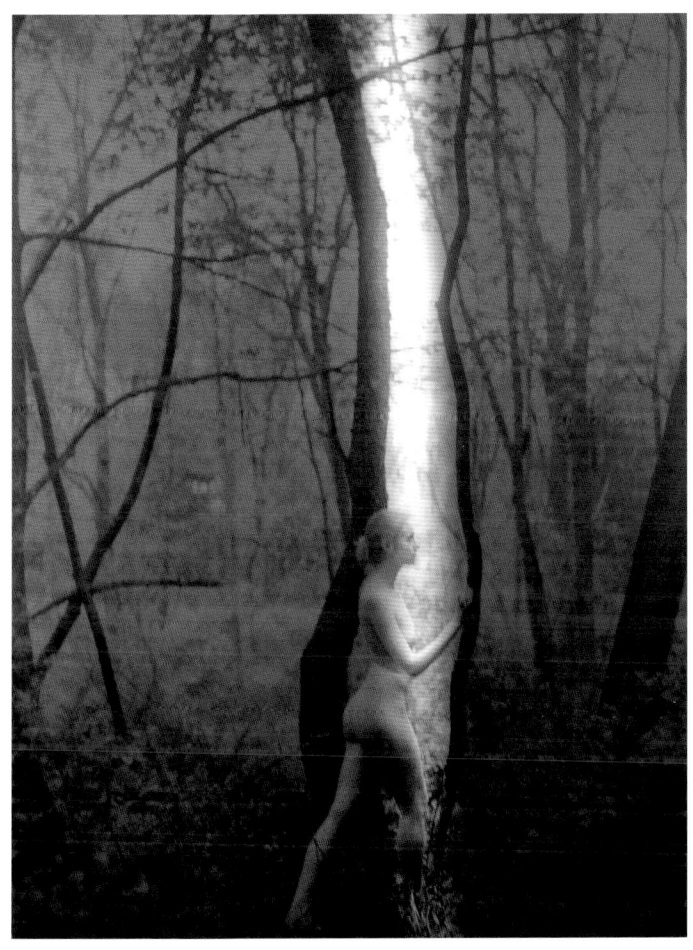

Her Power Arouses
or, Grasping the Nettle

by Jennifer Murray

In a contemporary landscape where highly fantasized and sexualized images of female bodies are entrenched in pornography and hyper-consumed online, it is often difficult to accept images of the female nude, maybe especially when made by female artists. When female bodies are involved, female artists are taken to task for embracing the tropes of the male gaze, but feminist narratives are continually evolving in response to our cultural moments. In our image-saturated culture, there remains a place for the nude as an agent for empowerment and revelation. Jordanna Kalman's *Little Romances* challenges the assumed power structures present in images of the female nude. Kalman pushes back against these assumptions, creating images depicting a subtle female sensuality that challenges the infantilized female sexuality that permeates conventional society. Moreover, in a cultural context where sexualized images of women are designed to belong to the viewer for their personal pleasure, Kalman's intimate narratives belong to her, the maker, and we are required to view them through her very specific lens.

Little Romances began as a reaction to the way her earlier, more conventional nudes were used and misappropriated online—often on pornography sites. In response, Kalman shifted her focus and began re-photographing

her work with the addition of objects, other photographs, or the inclusion of a rogue finger, making them
unsuitable or undesirable for porn sites. Allowing the
pictures to be both image and object allowed Kalman to
reassert her ownership and reclaim the photographs, as
well as, ultimately, the narrative of this series. Kalman
works with female figures metaphorically. The figure
is a stand-in for her personal experiences as a woman
and becomes a referent for a larger female experience in
contemporary culture—not overtly positive or negative,
but complicated.

Kalman has a tender approach to the female protag-
onists in her work, and we can see them gaining power
over time. In her prior series, *Invisible*, Kalman addresses
absence—feeling absent or missing from the world.
They are haunting images, with barely-there female
figures disappearing into the landscape or the wallpaper,
recalling Francesca Woodman's dissolving and erased
self-portraits. Where the *Invisible* images evoke loneliness,
later projects, such as *The Hole Sea*, begin to incorporate
mystical qualities, a reclaiming of feminine power in
the earthiest sense. *Little Romances* brings these threads
together; the women and girls here are more nuanced,
a mix of lonely and empowered, often divine and also
exceedingly normal. Their complexity as characters is

further problematized by the way we view them—as objects held in hand, with petals, branches, or bugs layered over parts of the image we are not allowed to see. This hiding and revealing of the figure conjures questions about the lines between shame and modesty, but also voyeurism and self-reflection, the monumental and the everyday. There is a new performative aspect to this series, but the performer is not the figure in the photograph: Kalman is. It's an interesting liminal breach—our role as the viewer has changed; these figures are not ours but rather hers, and we are allowed to view them at her discretion. She is interrupting our fantasy whether we like it or not.

Kalman's photographs emerge from a deeply personal and emotional place, one where she is continually questioning her own female experiences and the roles she is expected to play: wife, mother, daughter, lover, friend. Nature plays a role here too, both literally and figuratively. With the bits of plants, flowers, and insects that make their way onto the surface of the images, the relationship between woman and nature is explicit. This problematic connection is well documented by feminist scholars but continues to permeate our language. We still readily use gendered terms such as Mother Nature, and the iconography of Eve with her apple remains ubiquitous. Since the 1970s feminists and ecofeminists have been illuminating the negative connotations of the feminization of nature: When women are aligned with nature, their subjugation is implied, mirroring the way we subordinate and devalue the earth.[1] Little Romances doesn't erode that problem so much as illustrate it, and allows the viewer a glimpse into the psyche of a woman who endures prescribed social mores. The physical and emotional layers of these images address intimate female complexities, both the constraints of an idealized sexuality and a more complicated sensuality emanating from what women want for themselves instead of what they are wanted for. Here a woman is allowed to be whatever she wants—covered and exposed, mother and lover, mystical and mundane.

Instead of presenting the female as object for a male gaze, now the photograph itself takes on its own objecthood and becomes a kind of collected and cherished object. (A photograph is always an object, but we tend to forget this.) There are images within images, torn edges, flares of light, and surreal undertakings in the woods. The image is often imperfect, manipulated, collaged with elements not found in the primary scene. And a finger or a thumb jutting in from the corner leaves the

1. Catherine M. Roach, *Mother/Nature: Popular Culture and Environmental Ethics* (Bloomington: Indiana University Press, 2003), 37-38.

viewer wondering to whom these images belong: Who has collected these pictures, reworked them, and re-photographed them? Now the images have a physicality. Someone is holding them, touching them. Now they are truly objects, but they are Jordanna Kalman's objects, not ours. Individually each image is its own small narrative, but their collection in book form is a curated experience, a journey that Kalman controls.

It is hard to say that these images are sex- or body-positive or that they reject antiquated and prescribed concepts of the feminine—they are far too complicated for those specific messages. These narratives are more about questioning what it means to be female at this precise moment in the cultural complex, which is fully immersed in the virtual capitalism of pornography but also in the tension and empowerment of contemporary feminist discourse. In *Little Romances*, Kalman acknowledges a female experience that is fraught with both acceptance and anger for the role she plays in her own life.

Jennifer Murray is a curator, artist, and educator. She is the executive director of Filter Photo in Chicago and an instructor at Loyola University Chicago in the Department of Fine and Performing Arts.

Plate List

Acknowledgements

My love and gratitude to everyone who has been a part of this series:

Für die ausserordentliche und wunderschöne Constance Ausrine, Vielen Dank dass du Teil meines Lebens und meiner Arbeit bist. Du bedeutest mir sehr viel. Ich freue mich darauf wieder zusammen Pilze sammeln zu gehen, hoffentlich mit einem Adler der über uns wacht.

My beautiful loves Odile and Luna

Jesse Koechling

Rebecca Cairns, Juan Madrid, Jennifer Murray, Ursula Damm, Elizabeth Bell, Michael Itkoff, everyone at Daylight, Tabitha Ashura, Jen Ervin, everyone who contributed via Kickstarter & everyone who supported the campaign on social media, Fotofilmic, Aline Smithson, Lenscratch, Float Magazine, Ain't Bad, Brian Henry, Andrew Janjigian, Anna Malina

Thank you to my wonderful family:

John Cribbs
Robert and Linda Kalman
Pam and Mike Cribbs

Special thanks to my Dad, who introduced me to photography early on, has been incredibly generous with his knowledge, time, and equipment, and has been supportive even when I make "difficult art."